Cloverleaf

William K. Durr
Jean M. LePere
Mary Lou Alsin
Ruth Patterson Bunyan
Susan Shaw

CONSULTANT Paul McKee

HOUGHTON MIFFLIN COMPANY • Boston

Atlanta • Dallas • Geneva, Illinois • Hopewell, New Jersey • Palo Alto • Toronto

Acknowledgments

For each of the selections listed below, grateful acknowledgment is made for permission to adapt and/or reprint copyrighted material, as follows:

"After the Rain Is Over" is reprinted by permission of Charles Scribner's Sons from *In the Woods, In the Meadow, In the Sky.* Copyright © 1965 Aileen Fisher.

Alfred by Janice May Udry, adapted with permission of the publisher, copyright © 1960 by Albert Whitman and Company.

"Animals' Houses" by James Reeves. Reprinted by permission of William Heinemann Ltd., Publishers, from *The Wandering Moon* by James Reeves.

"Are We Lost, Daddy?" An adaptation of *Are We Lost, Daddy?* by Leonard Kessler. Copyright © 1967 by Grosset & Dunlap, Inc. Reprinted by permission of the publisher, Grosset & Dunlap, Inc.

"At the Top of My Voice" by Felice Holman. Reprinted from *At the Top of My Voice and Other Poems* by Felice Holman. Text copyright © 1970 by Felice Holman. Published by Grosset & Dunlap, Inc., New York. Reprinted by permission of the publisher.

The Bigger Giant retold by Nancy Green. Copyright © 1963 by Follett Publishing Company. Reprinted by permission of Follett Publishing Company, division of Follett Corporation.

"Bridges," from *Stories to Begin On* by Rhoda W. Bacmeister. Copyright © 1968 by Rhoda W. Bacmeister. Reprinted by permission of the publishers, E. P. Dutton & Co., Inc.

"Christina Katerina and the Box." Adapted by permission of Coward, McCann & Geoghegan, Inc. from *Christina Katerina and the Box* by Patricia Lee Gauch. Copyright © 1971 by Patricia Lee Gauch.

"City Rain," from *Taxis and Toadstools* by Rachel Field. Copyright 1962 by Doubleday and Company, Inc. Used by permission. British rights granted by World's Work Ltd.

"Moon Mouse," by Adelaide Holl. Adapted by permission of Random House, Inc. from *Moon Mouse*, by Adelaide Holl. Copyright © 1969 by Adelaide Holl.

"My Dog," by Emily Lewis. Reprinted from *Fives, Sixes, and Sevens: A Collection of Poetry for the Very Young,* compiled by Marjorie Stephenson, © 1969 by Fred-

erick Warne & Co., Inc. Extensive research failed to locate the author and/or the copyright owner of "My Dog."

"Nate the Great." Adapted by permission of Coward, McCann & Geoghegan, Inc. from *Nate the Great* by Marjorie Weinman Sharmat. Copyright © 1972 by Marjorie Weinman Sharmat.

"Parents Are People," by Carol Hall. From *Free to Be . . . You and Me,* by Marlo Thomas, et al., published by McGraw-Hill Book Company and the Ms. Foundation, Inc. Copyright © 1974 Free To Be Foundation Inc.

"Playtime in Africa," from poem beginning "Welcome, welcome rain" from *Playtime in Africa* by Efua Sutherland. Copyright © 1962 by Efua T. Sutherland and Willis E. Bell. Used by permission of Atheneum Publishers and Efua T. Sutherland. Published in England by Brown Knight & Truscott, Ltd.

"Riddles," by Ruth Ainsworth. Reprinted from *Fives, Sixes, and Sevens: A Collection of Poetry for the Very Young,* compiled by Marjorie Stephenson, © 1969 by Frederick Warne & Co., Inc. Reprinted by permission of Penguin Books Ltd. and Ruth Ainsworth.

"The Shoelaces," from *The Adventures of Mole and Troll* by Tony Johnston. Reprinted by permission of G. P. Putnam's Sons from *The Adventures of Mole and Troll* by Tony Johnston. Text copyright © 1972 by Tony Johnston; illustrations copyright © 1972 by Wallace Tripp.

"Troll Trick," by B. J. Lee. From *Poetry of Witches, Elves, and Goblins,* selected by Leland Blair Jacobs. Reprinted with the permission of Garrard Publishing Co., Champaign, Illinois. © 1970 by Leland B. Jacobs.

"You Do It Too," by Margaret Langford. Reprinted from *Fives, Sixes, and Sevens: A Collection of Poetry for the Very Young,* compiled by Marjorie Stephenson, © 1969 by Frederick Warne & Co., Inc. Reprinted by permission of Evans Brothers, Ltd.

What Mary Jo Shared by Janice May Udry, adapted with permission of the publisher, copyright © 1966 by Albert Whitman and Company.

Illustrators: PP. 101–119, MARC BROWN; P. 100, BILL CHARMATZ; PP. 38–43, CARY COCHRANE; PP. 159–175, PATRICIA COOMBS; P. 76, BEATRICE DARWIN; PP. 179–198, MIKE EAGLE; PP. 122–148, TOM EATON; P. 35, LEIGH GRANT; PP. 44–70, LEONARD KESSLER; PP. 36–37, 72–73, 120–121, 152–153, 204–205, TAD KRUMEICH; PP. 7–34, JOE MATHIEU; P. 206, IKKI MATSUMOTO; PP. 79–99, STELLA ORMAI; P. 176, SUSAN SWAN; P. 241, LYNN TITLEMAN; PP. 207–240, LORNA TOMEI; PP. 242–255, WALLACE TRIPP.

Photographers: P. 71, ERIK ANDERSON; P. 75, WILLIS E. BELL; PP. 156 (*center*), 158, IGNACIO FERNANDEZ; PP. 199 (*left*), 201 (*top left*), FRANKLIN PHOTO AGENCY; P. 201 (*lower left*), C. M. MONTGOMERY; PP. 199 (*top*), 203 (*left*), JOSEF MUENCH; PP. 201 (*center and right*), 202 (*center*), 203 (*right*), WILLIS PETERSON; PP. 155 (*top*), 157 (*center*), JIM RAYCROFT; PP. 154, 155, 156, 157 (*bottom*), 158, 256, GEORGE SHENG; PP. 149–151, FRANK SITEMAN; P. 241, BILL SUMNER; PP. 200 (*top*), 202 (*left*), L. W. WALKER, ARIZONA-SONORA DESERT MUSEUM.

Book cover and title page by MARILYN BASS *and* MARVIN GOLDMAN
Magazine covers by MARTUCCI STUDIO

Contents

Journeys

STORIES

POEMS

INFORMATIONAL ARTICLES

SKILL LESSONS

THE BIGGER GIANT

Retold by Nancy Green

Long, long ago there was a giant
named Fin McCool.

He was as big as a house, and his ears
were as big as pancakes.

Fin was strong.

He was so strong he could pick up
a big tree and make a walking stick of it.

Fin McCool was very big
and very strong.

Still, he was afraid of something.
But what would a giant be afraid of?
Only a bigger giant!

There was a giant named Cucullan
who was bigger than Fin McCool.
Not only was Cucullan bigger than Fin,
but he had a magic finger.

His magic finger made him very strong,
even stronger than Fin.

Cucullan had beaten every giant
but Fin McCool.

He told everyone
he was going to beat Fin, too,
just as soon as he could find him.

"That giant is so little I will only
have to hit him one time," said Cucullan.

So Fin was afraid.

Fin was big and strong,
but he was afraid of Cucullan.

One day Fin McCool told his wife
about Cucullan.
Fin's wife was very little.
She was so little she could sit
on Fin's head, but she was not afraid
of Cucullan.

"What can I do?" said Fin.
"Cucullan is mad!
He is as mad as a bear
with a bee in his ear.
He told all the giants
he was going to get me."

"Fin, Fin," said Fin's little wife.
"Don't be afraid of that Cucullan.
I'll help you."

"How can you help me?" said Fin.
"You are so little you can sit
on my head."

Fin's wife said, "I may be little,
but I can fool a giant."

"What if Cucullan comes today?"
said Fin.
"He has a magic finger.
Can you fool a giant who has
a magic finger?"

Fin's Wife Helps

"I will fool Cucullan," said Fin's wife.
"You wait and see.
I must make some cakes."

"But Cucullan is coming," said Fin.
"This is no time to be making cakes!"

"It's my cakes that will fool Cucullan,"
said Fin's wife.

As she made the cakes, Fin's wife
put a rock in each of them.

"How can we eat these cakes?" said Fin.

"Who wants to eat a cake
with a rock in it?"

"You wait and see," said his wife.

Then she made one more cake.
This cake did not have a rock in it.

"Good!" said Fin.
"There's a cake for a man to eat.
I will eat it."

"No, no!" said Fin's wife.

"Don't eat that cake.

That's the one

that will fool Cucullan."

"I don't like this," said Fin.

"How can a bit of a cake fool a giant

with a magic finger?"

"You wait and see," said his wife.

Fin looked out the window.

"Oh, help!" said Fin.
"I can see Cucullan.
He is coming after me now."

"Then it's time for you to get
into the baby's bed," said Fin's wife.

"What?" said Fin.
"What did you say?"

"You must get into the baby's bed,"
said Fin's wife.

"Giants do not get into baby beds,"
said Fin.

"It is a big baby bed," said Fin's wife.
"You must get into it
so we can fool Cucullan.
I will tell him you are Fin's baby boy."

So Fin took his shoes
and put them down.

Five cats jumped into his left shoe
and went to sleep.

Fin got into the bed.

It was a big bed, big enough
for a baby giant.

But Fin was not a baby giant.

He was a big giant.

So he could not get his feet in.

He did not fit at all
and was not at all happy.

Cucullan Comes

Fin shook in the bed.

He could hear Cucullan
coming up the hill.

That giant was so big
that everything shook as he walked.

"I don't like this," said Fin.

"Who ever saw a giant in a baby's bed?

How will this fool Cucullan?"

"You wait and see," said his wife.

Cucullan came to Fin's house.

Fin's wife went to the door.

Cucullan looked down at Fin's wife.

He had to look way down.

"Is this the house of Fin McCool?"
said Cucullan.

Fin's wife looked up at Cucullan.

She had to look way up.

"This is Fin McCool's house," she said.

"Is Fin McCool at home?"
said Cucullan.

"No. Fin McCool is not here,"
said Fin's wife.

"He has gone to look for a giant
named Cucullan.

I'm sorry for that giant."

Cucullan laughed.

His laugh was so big the house shook.

"I am Cucullan," he said.

"Do you see how big I am?

Are you sorry for me?"

Fin's wife looked up at Cucullan.

"You must look out for Fin," she said.

"Fin is big and strong."

Cucullan laughed.

"Is Fin McCool strong?" he said.

"That's not what I thought.

I'll show him who is really strong."

He laughed again.

Fin shook in the baby's bed.

He did not like the sound

of Cucullan's big laugh.

"The wind is banging the door,"
said Fin's wife.

"Could you help by turning
the house around so the wind
won't bang the door?

If Fin were here, he would do it."

Cucullan was surprised at that.
He didn't know that Fin could turn
a house around.

Cucullan pulled his magic finger
three times.

That made him very strong.

He took up the house
and turned it around.

It was hard work, but he did it.

"Can Fin McCool really do that?"
said Cucullan.

He was wondering if he wanted
to see this Fin McCool after all.

Something to Eat

"Would you like something to eat
after your hard work?" said Fin's wife.

"Yes, please," said Cucullan.

"I have some cake," said Fin's wife.
She gave Cucullan a cake
that had a rock in it.
He took a big bite of the cake.

"Yow!" said Cucullan.
"Oh! Oh! My teeth!
What kind of cake is this
you gave me?"

"That is Fin's cake," said his wife.

"Does Fin really eat that kind
of cake?" said Cucullan.

"Yes," said Fin's wife.

"Fin and his baby boy are
the only ones who can eat it.

But I thought you were strong
for a little man.

I thought you could eat it, too."

"Maybe I won't wait for Fin
to come back after all," said Cucullan.

"Oh, don't go," said Fin's wife.
"Here is another cake.
Maybe this one is not so hard."

He took a big bite of the cake.
"Yow! My teeth!" he said.
"This cake is as hard
as the other one."

"Don't make so much noise
about it," said Fin's wife.
"The baby is asleep."

Fin's wife looked at Fin
in the baby's bed.

"Wa-a-a-a," cried Fin.

"You did it," said Fin's wife
to Cucullan.
"Now I'll have to give the baby
something to eat."

Cucullan and Baby Fin

She took the cake that did not have
a rock in it and gave it to Fin.

Fin took three big bites
and the cake was gone.

Cucullan said, "What a baby!
"How could a baby eat a cake like that?
That cake broke two of my teeth."

"He's a big strong boy,"
said Fin's wife.

"Someday he may be as strong
as his daddy Fin.

Feel his teeth, little man.

You will find they are very strong."

"Let me feel your teeth, baby,"
said Cucullan.

"His teeth are far back in his head,"
said Fin's wife.
"You must put your finger far in."

So Cucullan put his finger far in.
He was surprised to find teeth so strong
in a baby.

What do you think Fin did then?

He bit Cucullan's magic finger.

"Oh, help! My magic finger!

I'm not going to wait for Fin McCool,"
said Cucullan.

"Fin's baby boy is enough for me."

And he ran out the door.

He ran away from Fin's house
as fast as he could go.

Fin and his wife laughed.

Fin looked down at his little wife
and said, "You really did fool that giant.
He's gone, and I don't think
we will ever see him again."

And Fin McCool was right.
Never again did Cucullan come
to see Fin or Fin's wife or Fin's baby boy.

At the Top of My Voice

When I stamp
The ground thunders,
When I shout
The world rings,
When I sing
The air wonders
How I do such things.

— Felice Holman

Two Sounds *a* Can Stand For

■Listen for the vowel sound in each of these words as you say it to yourself.

man   take   hard   fall

Each of those words has the vowel **a** in it.

But no two of those words have the same vowel sound, do they?

The vowel **a** doesn't stand for just one sound.

By itself or with another vowel, it can stand for any one of many sounds.

■Listen for the vowel sound in each of these words as you say it to yourself.

cake   name   gave

The vowel sound you hear in each of those words is the same as the name of the letter **a**, isn't it?

We call that sound the long **a** sound.

Do you hear the long **a** sound in each
of these words?

way   rain   play

■The squirrels are looking for words
with the long **a** sound in them.

Can you help the squirrels?

▧Now listen for the vowel sound
in each of these words.

back   pan   cat

The vowel sound you hear in each
of those words is just like
the first sound in **am**, isn't it?

We call that sound the short **a** sound.

Do you hear the short **a** sound
in each of these words?

raccoon   ladder   happy

■The bees want to find words that
have the short **a** sound in them.

See if you can help the bees.

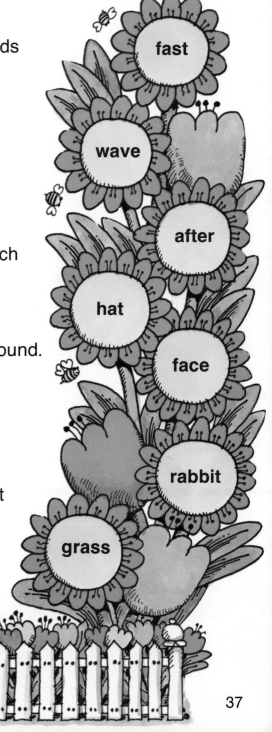

fast

wave

after

hat

face

rabbit

grass

READING A MAP

A map shows where places are.
If you know how to read a map,
you can get to those places.

Let's look at this map.
Find Park Road.

Three roads cross Park Road.
What are the names of these roads?

One road on this map
is much bigger than the other roads.
This road is called a highway.

Many cars go on this big highway.
The highway goes by a mountain.
What is the name of that mountain?

Find the valley on the map.
What is the name of the valley?

There are farms in the valley.
Many of the farms have barns
and farm animals.
But you can't see the barns and
the animals on this map.

Maps can't show everything.

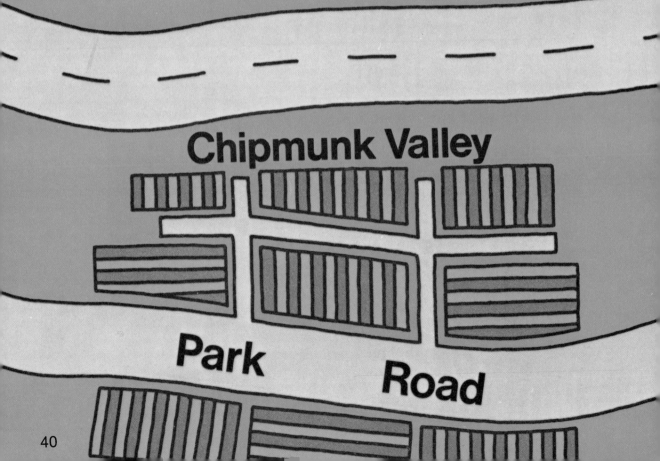

Chipmunk Valley

Park

Road

The highway goes by Chipmunk Valley.

If you drove on the highway
by Chipmunk Valley,
what would you come to?
You would come to a city.
Its name is New City.

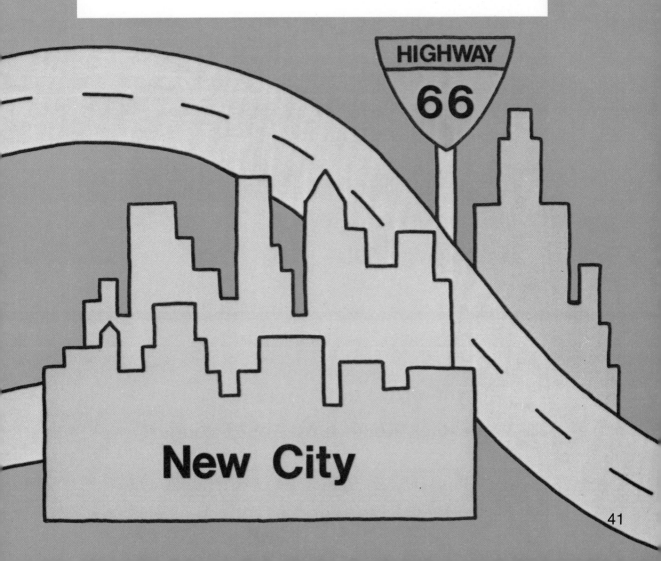

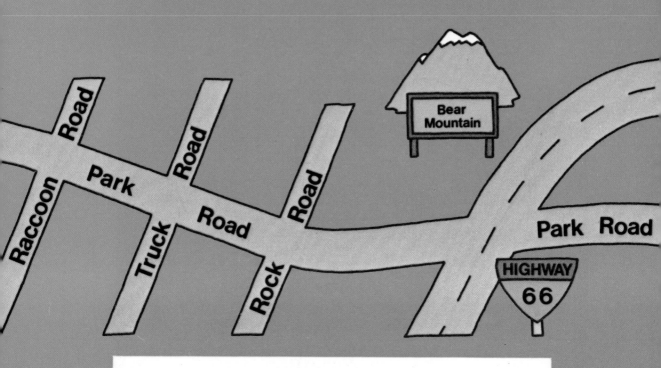

Look at the map now!
You can see ALL the places.

You can see that Park Road goes
across the highway
and into the valley.

You can see Bear Mountain
and New City at the same time.

If you drove to Chipmunk Valley
from Rock Road, how would you go?

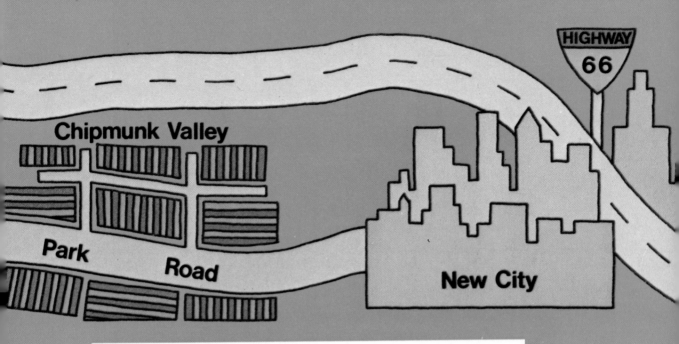

Chipmunk Valley

Park Road

New City

HIGHWAY 66

You would go on Park Road
across to the valley.

If you lived on Raccoon Road,
how would you get to Bear Mountain?
You would take Park Road
to the big highway and turn left
to Bear Mountain.

And you wouldn't get lost.
Why not?
You know how to read your map!

Are We Lost, Daddy?

by Leonard Kessler

"Is everyone ready?" asked Father.

"We are ready," said Mother.
"We are ready to go to Big Valley.
All five suitcases are here."

"Let's see," said Father.
"Did you turn out all the lights?"

"Yes," said Mother.
"I turned out the lights.
Did you close all the windows?"

"Yes," said Father.
"And I locked all the doors."

Mother smiled and said,
"We didn't forget anything."

"Then it looks as if we are ready
to go," said Father.
"Are the children ready?"

"We are ready," called the children.

Father, Mother, the boy, the girl,
the cat, and the dog all got
into the car.

"Make sure you lock your doors
and put on your seat belts,"
said Mother.

"We are off," said Father.
"Off to Big Valley."

Away they went.

Look at all those cars!

Look at all those trucks!

Look at all those signs!

HONK!
HONK!

DORIS
DRESSES

48

"I'm hungry!" said the boy.

"Let's eat!" said the girl.

"You just ate," said Mother.

"You will have to wait a little before we eat," said Father.
"I want to get off this busy road. I think I will take the back roads. It's more fun to go that way, and there are not as many cars on the road."

"But are you SURE that you know
the way?" asked Mother.
"It was a long time ago
that we went to Big Valley."

"I KNOW the way!
I KNOW the way!" said Father.
He turned the car off the highway
and onto a back road.

"Be sure to read all the signs.
We don't want to get lost,"
said Mother.

50

On the Back Road

"Are we lost, Daddy?"
asked the children.

"No, we are not lost," said Father.
"I know the way.
First I must go past a big red barn
with a yellow door.
That is where I make a left turn."

Father drove and drove.
He did not find the barn
with the yellow door.

"Why don't you stop and ask someone
if this is the right way?" asked Mother.

"I KNOW the way!" said Father.
He drove and drove for five more miles.
But he did not see a big red barn
with a yellow door.

He saw a farmer.
"I will stop and ask the farmer
about that barn," said Father.

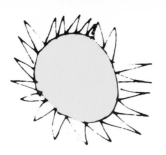

He stopped the car.
"Is this the way to Big Valley?
I know I must go past
a big red barn," said Father.

"Would that be a big red barn
with a yellow door?" asked the farmer.

"THAT'S THE BARN!" said Father.

The farmer smiled.
"Oh, they painted that barn white!
You went past it about ten miles back,"
he said.

"Oh, no!" cried Father.

"Now we must go back ten miles."

"You don't have to do that,"
said the farmer.

"You just go up this hill
and down the hill.

Turn left at a little red schoolhouse.

Go west about five miles,
and you will be on the road
to Big Valley.

You can't miss it."

"Thank you very much," said Father.

High on a Mountain

Father drove up the hill.

He went down the hill.

He turned left

at the little red schoolhouse.

He went west for five miles.

And where was he?

On top of a high mountain!
No Big Valley here.
"Are we lost, Daddy?"
asked the children.

"No, we are not lost," said Father.
"We are on top of a high mountain!"
Down the mountain he drove.

He saw a woman working.
He stopped the car.
"How do I get to Big Valley?"
he asked.

"Big Valley? Hmm..." said the woman.

"You go south on this road.

Go up a hill and down a hill.

When you come to a long white fence,
turn right.

Then you will be on the road
to Big Valley.

You can't miss it."

"Thank you very much," said Father.

And off he went.

Up a hill and down a hill.

He came to a white fence.

He turned left.

He drove ten miles.

And where was the car?

The car was stuck.

It was stuck in a muddy road.

No Big Valley here.

"I'm hungry," said the boy.

"I want some water," said the girl.

The dog barked.

The cat cried, "Meow!"

What a lot of noise!

"Are you sure you know
where you are?" asked Mother.

"Sure I know where I am,"
said Father.

"I am stuck in the mud!"

Stuck in the Mud

They all got out of the car.

"Everyone push when I say three,"
said Father.

"Ready? One . . . two . . . THREE! PUSH!"

The car was still stuck in the mud.

"What can we do now?" asked Mother.

"I'm hungry," said the boy.

"I want some water," said the girl.

The dog barked.

"Meow!" cried the cat.

A man drove by in a truck.

"Can I help you?" he asked.

"Oh, yes," said Father.
"We are stuck in the mud."

"Then I will help you," said the man.

First he did this:

Then he did this:

Around and around went the big wheels
of the truck.
The car moved out of the mud.

"Thank you. Thank you,"
said Father.

"Do you know the way
to Big Valley?" he asked.

"Oh, yes," said the man.
"You go up the hill
and down the hill.

Turn left at the first STOP sign.

Go five miles north,
and there you will find the road
to Big Valley.

You can't miss it."

Father got into the car.

He went up a hill and down a hill.

He made a left turn at the STOP sign.

He drove north for five miles.

And where do you think he was?

"I think I've seen this before,"
said Father.

"Yes, you have," said Mother.

"You are back where you began.

Back at the farmer's house."

"Oh, no, no, NO!" cried Father.

"Are we lost, Daddy?"
asked the children.

"No, you are not lost," said Father.

I AM LOST!

They saw a boy walking along the road.

"Do you know the way to Big Valley?"
asked Father.

"No, I don't know the way
to Big Valley," said the boy.

"You DON'T know the way?"
said Father.

"You are the first one we have asked
today who did not know the way."

"But I know what you can do,"
said the boy.

"Get a map."

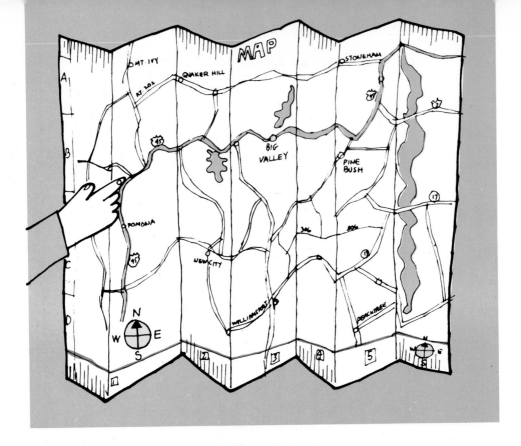

A Map at Last

"The map will show you the best way
to get to Big Valley," said the boy.

"A MAP!" said Father.
"I will stop and get a map."
And that is what he did.

"Look at this map," said Father.
"First, let's find out where we are
on the map."

"First we must hold it the right way.
You are holding the map upside down,"
said Mother.

"Oh," said Father.
He turned the map around.
"Here is where we are," said Father.
"And here is Big Valley!
We just go along this road
until we get to Big Valley."

"We are off," said Mother.

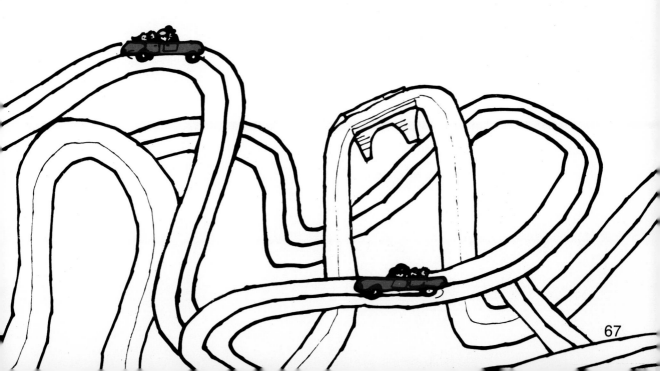

"We are off to Big Valley!"
cried the children.
Father drove and drove.
He drove up a hill
and down a hill,
past a barn, past a farm,
and over a mountain,
until he came to BIG VALLEY!

"We are here," said the boy.
"I'm hungry."

"We are here," said the girl.
"I want some water."

"We are here," said Mother.
"At last!"

A man stopped his car.

He asked Father,

"How do I get to New City?

What is the best way to go?"

"Hmmm . . ." said Father.

He smiled.

"The best way to go to New City

is to stop and get a MAP.

That is the best way!

You can't miss it!"

THE END

BRIDGES

— Rhoda W. Bacmeister

I like to look for bridges
Everywhere I go,
Where the cars go over
With water down below.

Standing by the railings
I watch the water slide
Smoothly under to the dark,
And out the other side.

71

Two Sounds *e* Can Stand For

■Listen for the vowel sound in each of these words as you say it to yourself.

bed   be   her   bear

Each of those words has the vowel **e** in it.

But no two of those words have the same vowel sound, do they?

The vowel **e** doesn't stand for just one sound.

By itself or with another vowel, it can stand for any one of many sounds.

■Listen for the vowel sound in each of these words as you say it to yourself.

he   tree   reach

The vowel sound you hear in each of those words is the same as the name of the letter **e**, isn't it?

We call that sound the long **e** sound.

each

green

let

feet

best

she

eat

help

bee

new

Do you hear the long **e** sound in each of these words?

these   she   feel

■The signs with long **e** words on them show the way to the city.

See if you can find those signs.

■Now listen for the vowel sound in each of these words.

yes   tell   when

The vowel sound you hear in each of those words is just like the first sound in **end**, isn't it?

We call that sound the short **e** sound.

Do you hear the short **e** sound in each of these words?

better   yellow   every

■The trucks with short **e** words on them are new.

Find the new trucks.

73

PLAYTIME IN AFRICA

Welcome, welcome rain.

The trees and I were waiting for you.

You stayed away so long,

   all through December, January, February.

Now the trees and I can wash and drink.

And something the trees can't do,

   I can do.

I can run and splash and play

   in dancing puddles everywhere.

— Efua Sutherland

75

CITY RAIN

Rain in the city!
   I love to see it fall
Slantwise where the buildings crowd
   Red brick and all.
Streets of shiny wetness
   Where the taxis go,
With people and umbrellas all
   Bobbing to and fro.

           — *Rachel Field*

Discoveries

STORIES

POEMS

SKILL LESSONS

PLAY

MOON MOUSE

by Adelaide Holl

One night Mother Mouse called
to her baby.

"Come, Arthur," she said.

"Now that you are old enough,
you may stay up after dark.

Let us look at the night sky."

Arthur ran happily to the door
of the nest and looked out.

The black sky was all around him.

Darkness was everywhere.

The night was still and cool.

Arthur could feel the coolness
on his little nose.

He could feel it on his whiskers
and his round little ears.

"So this is what the night is like!"
he said happily.

"It is wonderful!"

Arthur looked up.
There in the blackness
was something
    big and round
        and shining.
"Look!" he cried in excitement.
"Oh, look! Look!"

Mother Mouse smiled.
"It is only the moon," she said.
"It is the big, round, yellow moon."

"Where is the moon?" asked Arthur,
his bright eyes shining.

"Very far away," his mother told him.
"Up, up, high in the sky."

"What is it for?" asked the little mouse.

Mother Mouse said, "It shines
in the dark.
It gives us light."

"What is it made of?" asked Arthur
in excitement.

"I do not know," said his mother.
"I have heard that it is made of cheese,
but I do not think so."

"I would like to go there," said Arthur.
"I would like to go to the moon."

His mother smiled.
"Not tonight," she said.
"Come. It is bedtime."

Off to the Moon

Arthur thought about the moon.
He thought about it day after day.
He thought about it night after night.

"How far away is the moon?"
he asked his mother one day.

"Very, very far," she told him.
"Farther than any place
you've seen.
Farther than the meadow.
Farther than the farmer's cornfield.
Farther than the fields
of golden wheat."

One night, Arthur said to himself,
"I am old enough to stay up after dark.
I must be old enough
to go to the moon."

He looked up.
The sky was dark and cloudy.
He could not see
the round, yellow moon anywhere.
"I will go look for the moon,"
said Arthur to himself.

So he went off all alone.

He went a long, long way —

past the meadow,

past the farmer's cornfield,

past the fields of golden wheat.

On and On

The sky was black and cloudy.

Then, little by little, the stars began
to come out.

Arthur went on and on
until he came to a place
with many lights
and many noises
and many buildings.

And there, all at once, he saw
the moon sitting at the very top
of a high building.

He looked about in excitement.

He saw steps going up and up and up.

"This must be the way to the moon,"
he said.

So he began to climb.

He climbed until he could go no higher.

And there he saw an open place
for going in.

"This must be the door to the moon,"
he said to himself.

And he went in.

Sure enough!
Inside was something
    big
        and round
           and yellow.
And it was made of cheese!

"It is the moon!" cried Arthur,
his eyes big and shining.

He skipped all about.

He ran in and out of the little holes.

He nibbled a bit here.

He nibbled a bit there.

At last, he was very full
and very tired!

"The moon is a delicious place,"
he said to himself.

"But I think I will go home now."

He
climbed
down,
all the way down
to the ground.

He went a long, long way —
past the fields of golden wheat,

past the farmer's cornfield,

past the meadow.

He went all the way home to his nest.

Home Again

"Where have you been?"
asked Mother Mouse.
"I have been looking for you."

"I have been all the way to the moon,"
said Arthur in excitement.
"It <u>is</u> big and round and yellow.
It <u>is</u> made of cheese.
And it is very delicious!"

Mother Mouse smiled.
"Funny little mouse!" she said kindly.

Arthur looked up at the night sky.

A light rain was falling.

There was darkness all about.

"Where is the moon?"
he asked his mother.

"It is a rainy, cloudy night,"
she told him.

"The moon is hiding."

Arthur looked for the moon
the next night, and again the next.
Night after night he waited.
But there was only the blackness
and the rain.

Then one night, the rain stopped.
All at once, the moon came out.
It was shiny.
It was bright.
But it was not big and round.
It was only a small bit of the moon.
One side of the moon was missing.

"Look!" Arthur called to his mother
in excitement.

"See what a lot of the moon I nibbled!"

"So you did," said his mother
with a smile.

"It is a good thing you did not
eat it all up!"

RiDDLES

What thing am I?

1   I have legs,
One, two, three, four
But I cannot walk
Across the floor.

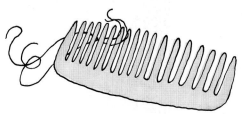

2   I have teeth
Long and white,
They are sharp
But I cannot bite.

3   I am round like a ball
And I live in the sky,
You will see me at night
If you look up high.

1 and 2 — Ruth Ainsworth   3 — Anonymous

The King's New Pet

by Mary Lou Alsin

Castle

The **People** are you children who watch the play.

King

Dick Unicorn

Rick Unicorn

Nick Unicorn

Mother Cat

Kitten

Old Fisherman

Boy

Outside the Castle
(The king is in a big golden chair.)

KING: Good morning, people of Woo.

Good morning, unicorns.

Today is the big unicorn race.

PEOPLE: Hooray! Hooray!

DICK UNICORN: Today the king
will find the best unicorn.
That unicorn will live in the castle.

RICK UNICORN: He will go everywhere
with the king.
That unicorn will take the king
all over Woo.
The king will find out
how his people are getting along.

KING: I want the unicorn that is best
in every way for a pet.

DICK UNICORN: I'm the best.
I'm great and my long legs
make me the fastest unicorn.
I have to win.

RICK UNICORN: I am great!
My coat is white.
And my horn is long.
I am the best-looking unicorn.
I should be the one to take
the king all over Woo.

DICK UNICORN: Oh, look, Rick!
Here comes Nick!

KING: Unicorns, get ready!
The race will start here.

DICK UNICORN: Nick, you can't win
this race.
You can't even run fast.

106

RICK UNICORN: Nick, you shouldn't run
in the race.
Look at your terrible horn.
It isn't like a unicorn's horn
at all.

NICK UNICORN: I may not win this race.
But the king wants us all to run,
so I'll do the best I can.

KING: All unicorns, please come
to the starting place.

KING: Rocks painted red will show
you the way.
You will run uphill and downhill.
You will run around the big pond.
You will run along the road
that goes to the dark woods.
When you get to the woods,
you will turn around and come
straight back here.
Are you ready?
One . . . Two . . . Three . . . GO!

108

At the Top of the Last Hill

DICK UNICORN: I've made it up every hill.

I'm happy this is the last one.

I would cry if there were more hills.

MOTHER CAT: Help! Help!

DICK UNICORN: I can't stop now,

Mother Cat.

I must run fast.

I want to win this race.

I'll show the king I'm the best.

RICK UNICORN: Here I am at last.
I'm thankful there are no more hills.

MOTHER CAT: Help! Help!

RICK UNICORN: Oh, I can't stop now,
Mother Cat.
I'd get my white coat dirty.
I want the king to make me his pet.

NICK UNICORN: I'm still running last.
But I'm doing better than I thought
I would.
This must be the last hill!

MOTHER CAT: Help! Help!

NICK UNICORN: Oh, I must help
the poor mother cat.

MOTHER CAT: My little kitten
has climbed out there.
He can't get down!
I'm afraid
he will be hurt.

111

NICK UNICORN: I'll help you.

Your kitten will be all right.

I'll pull the tree over with my horn.

MOTHER CAT: Thank you! Thank you!

NICK UNICORN: I'm in a race.

I must go now. Good-by!

112

The Pond

DICK UNICORN: Here's the pond.

OLD FISHERMAN: Help! Help!

DICK UNICORN: I have no time for you,
Old Fisherman!
I have to get all the way
around the pond as fast as I can.

RICK UNICORN: Good! There's the pond.
And Dick's just ahead of me.

OLD FISHERMAN: Help! Help!

RICK UNICORN: Not now, Old Fisherman!
I can't get into the water.
My coat would look terrible.

NICK UNICORN: The pond, at last!

OLD FISHERMAN: Help! Help!

NICK UNICORN: Dick and Rick are way
ahead of me.
But I have to help
the poor old fisherman.

OLD FISHERMAN: There are too many
big fish in my net.
Will you help me lift it out of the water?

NICK UNICORN: I'll help you.
I will even empty the net for you.

OLD FISHERMAN: Thank you! Thank you!

NICK UNICORN: I must get going.

The Woods

DICK UNICORN: The woods at last!
Now I must run straight back
to the castle.

BOY: Help! Help!
I'm stuck in a mudhole.

DICK UNICORN: I can't help you now.
I'm about to win a race.
Make way for the winner!

RICK UNICORN: Hooray! The woods!

BOY: Help! Help!
I'm stuck in a mudhole.

RICK UNICORN: Help you out of that mud!
I'd get mud all over me.
And I wouldn't even win the race.

NICK UNICORN: Here are the woods.
Now I have to run back to the castle.

BOY: Help! Help!
I'm stuck in a mudhole.

NICK UNICORN: Just when I thought
I could win.
But I must help the poor boy.

BOY: Oh, thank you!

NICK UNICORN: I have to be on my way.
I can't win the race now.
But I'm happy I could help.

Back at the Castle

KING: Hooray! Hooray!

PEOPLE: Hooray! Hooray!

KING: The three unicorns are back.
I wanted to find the fastest runner . . .

DICK UNICORN: I'm the winner!

KING: But fast legs aren't everything.
I wanted a unicorn who was fast
and good looking, too.

RICK UNICORN: Oh, that's me!
I'm the winner!

KING: But the longest horn
and the whitest coat
don't always make the best unicorn.
Most of all I wanted a unicorn
that was friendly and kind.
Dick, did you help a cat,
a fisherman, or a boy?

DICK UNICORN: Not me.
I just didn't have time.

KING: And what about you, Rick?

RICK UNICORN: I couldn't do that.
I was afraid I'd get dirty.

KING: Did you help anyone, Nick?

NICK UNICORN: Yes, when someone wants
help, I do what I can.
That's why I lost the race.

KING: Lost the race!
You're the winner.
You're great!
I asked the cat, the fisherman,
and the boy to find the unicorn
most willing to help others.
Nick, you are that unicorn.
You are the king's new pet!

PEOPLE: Hooray for Nick! Hooray!

119

Two Sounds *i* Can Stand For

■Listen for the vowel sound in each of these words as you say it to yourself.

fish   bird   mile   field

Each of those words has the vowel **i** in it.

But no two of those words have the same vowel sound, do they?

The vowel **i** doesn't stand for just one sound.

By itself or with another vowel, it can stand for any one of many sounds.

■Listen for the vowel sound in each of these words as you say it to yourself.

time   kind   high

The vowel sound you hear in each of those words is the same as the name of the letter **i** isn't it?

We call that sound the long **i** sound.

Do you hear the long **i** sound in each
of these words?

side   **bite**   **like**

■ Little Bear wants to get the fish
with long **i** words on them.

Can you help Little Bear?

■ Now listen for the vowel sound
in each of these words.

pick   **sit**   **didn't**

The vowel sound you hear in each
of those words is just like
the first sound in **is**, isn't it?

We call that sound the short **i** sound.

Do you hear the short **i** sound in each
of these words?

chipmunk   **picture**   **nibbled**

■ Little Bear wants to find the pans
that have the short **i** words on them.

See if you can help Little Bear
find those pans.

five

this

hide

big   kitten   dirty

121

ALFRED

by Janice Udry

Henry was afraid of dogs.

It did no good for Father to say,
"It's silly for you to be afraid, Henry.
The dog is the kindest animal of all."

And it didn't help when his mother said,
"Dogs will not hurt you, Henry."

Henry was afraid of dogs. ALL dogs.

Henry's home was
on a very doggy street.

Every day, by himself, he had to go
past all the dogs to get to school.

When Henry thought about the walk
past them, he could not even eat
his breakfast.

Henry liked eggs.
He liked toast with honey.
But when he thought about the dogs,
he just didn't like eggs and toast,
or even honey, any more.

When he left for school,
Henry never waved to his mother
in the window.

He just looked straight ahead
and began walking down the street
like a wind-up toy.

The first dog he came to was
a big white poodle named Ko-Ko.

Every morning Ko-Ko watched for Henry
and began barking as soon as he saw him.

"It's good that he's fenced in!"
thought Henry as he went past.
He never looked at Ko-Ko.

Before Ko-Ko had stopped barking,
Henry came to another dog.

This was a mean-looking bulldog
named Butch.

He barked even more than Ko-Ko.

He was not fenced in his yard.

But he had never come out
into the street after Henry.

Every day Henry thought
that Butch was going to come out.

And to Henry this was just as bad
as if he had.

There were still more dogs
that Henry had to go past every day.

One was an old dog named Mary.

Another was a little dog
named Carmichael.

Every day Mary and Carmichael
watched for Henry.
They barked at him for as long as
they could see him.

The noise on Henry's street
every morning was terrible.

Then Came Alfred!

Last of all, Henry came to the dog that scared him the most.

This was Alfred, a giant brown dog!
He was the most terrible dog.
He came right up to Henry.
He even jumped on him!

When Henry came to Alfred's yard,
he always began to run.
He ran all the way to school.

"Your face is so red, Henry.
You mustn't play so hard,"
said Miss Miller.

She didn't know
why his face was so red.

Poor Henry!
Every day the same street,
the same terrible walk,
and the same cross, barking dogs.

Then the most terrible thing of all happened.

Something that Henry had always been afraid would happen.

He left for school.

He went past Ko-Ko and Butch, then past Mary and Carmichael.

They barked at him as they always did.

Henry looked straight ahead as he always did.

He saw Alfred waiting.

When Alfred saw Henry, he ran
straight out at him.
Alfred jumped up.

He looked so terrible
that Henry dropped his schoolbag.

Alfred took the schoolbag in his teeth
and ran down the street.
He even looked as if he were laughing.

Henry could just watch him go.
He would never go after Alfred
and make him give back the schoolbag.

Henry thought sadly
about his very first schoolbag.
Now he would never get it back.
But Henry would not cry.

"My schoolbag has been taken,"
he told Miss Miller when he got to school.

"Taken?" said Miss Miller.
"Are you sure, Henry?"

"Yes," said Henry.
"Alfred took my schoolbag
this morning."

Henry didn't want Miss Miller to ask
who Alfred was, but she did.

"Who is Alfred?" asked Miss Miller.

Henry didn't like to tell her about Alfred
and how he was afraid of him.

"Alfred is a dog. A very big dog,"
said Henry.

"And he took your schoolbag, Henry?
Then, after school you must go
to Alfred's house," said Miss Miller.

"Just ask the people who own Alfred
if they have seen your schoolbag."

Then Miss Miller told the children
that it was time to sing.

But Henry couldn't sing.

The idea of going into Alfred's yard
and up to the door where he lived
made Henry terribly afraid.

How could he make himself do that?

A Sound at the Door

Henry sat by the door.

He was the first to hear

the funny noise at the door.

It was really two sounds,

a scratch-scratch and a sniff-sniff.

Henry looked at Miss Miller,

but she was singing with the children

and didn't hear the noise.

Then the door began to open.

Henry looked.

Through the opening came a dog's nose.

Alfred's nose!

Through the door
came Alfred's big head.

And in his teeth was Henry's schoolbag!

Alfred pushed the door open
and stood looking all around.

He didn't see Henry.

Alfred looked at Miss Miller
and wagged his tail.

Henry thought Alfred looked
even bigger in the schoolroom
than he did outdoors.

Then Miss Miller looked up
and saw Alfred.
She stopped singing.
The children stopped singing, too.

"A dog!" one of the children shouted.
"Look, Miss Miller, a big dog."

The children were standing up to look,
and some of them began to laugh.
But Henry was stuck to his seat.

Miss Miller said, "Good morning.
Could it be that you are Alfred?"

At the sound of his name,
Alfred wagged his tail.
"Alfred has brought your schoolbag,
Henry," said Miss Miller.

Alfred saw Henry then
and went over to his seat.

"What if he jumps on me?"
thought Henry.

Alfred put the schoolbag
right in front of Henry.
Then he sat down beside Henry.

"Is that your dog?" asked Sammy.

"He just lives on my street,"
said Henry.

"Did you thank him, Henry?"
asked Miss Miller.

"He didn't mean to take
your schoolbag this morning."

Henry looked at his schoolbag.
It looked as good as ever.

Then he looked at Alfred and saw
something that he had never seen before.
He saw Alfred's eyes.
They were soft and brown.
But what Henry was surprised to see
was that Alfred's eyes were sad.

My Friend Alfred

When Henry saw those sad eyes,
he wasn't afraid of Alfred any more.

He said something to Alfred
for the first time.
"Thank you, Alfred.
Thank you for giving back
my schoolbag."
He hugged Alfred's big head.

Alfred wagged his tail,
but he did not move.
His sad, brown eyes became happy.
He had wanted Henry to like him.

Miss Miller let Alfred stay in school.
Every time Henry looked up
from his schoolwork, he saw Alfred
sitting beside him.

When it was time to go home,
Henry felt good walking out the door
with Alfred close beside him.

The other children watched them turn
onto Henry's street.

When they came to Alfred's house,
Henry said, "Good-by, Alfred.
I'll see you in the morning."

But Alfred just wagged his tail
and walked past his own yard.

Mary and Carmichael were barking
and waiting for Henry to come by.
When they saw Alfred walking
beside Henry, they stopped barking.
They were afraid of Alfred.

Butch, the bulldog, was waiting, too.

But when he saw Alfred,

he ran inside his doghouse.

Then they came to Ko-Ko's yard.

"Where is Ko-Ko?" wondered Henry.

Then he saw him.

Ko-Ko had seen Alfred with Henry.

He was hiding under a bush

in his yard.

He watched Henry and Alfred go past

without barking at all.

Henry and Alfred went up the walk
to Henry's house.

When Henry's mother came to the door,
Henry said, "This is my friend, Alfred."

"Hello, Alfred," said Henry's mother.
"I am very happy to know you."

Alfred wagged his tail
and lifted up one paw.
Mother took his paw in her hand.

Then Alfred turned and went
down the walk.
He went back to his own house.

The next morning Henry ate three eggs
and some toast with honey.

He was very hungry.

He said good-by to his mother
and took his schoolbag in his hand.

He went out the door.

There was Alfred, just as
Henry thought he would be, waiting.

"Oh, good morning, Alfred," said Henry,
hugging Alfred's big head.

"I am so happy to see you!"

Henry waved to his mother.
His mother waved back.
Then Henry and Alfred went to school.

My Dog

Have you seen a little dog
   anywhere about?
A raggy dog, a shaggy dog,
   who's always looking out
For some fresh mischief which he thinks
   he really ought to do.
He's very likely, at this minute,
   biting someone's shoe.

If you see that little dog,
  his tail up in the air,
A whirly tail, a curly tail,
  a dog who doesn't care
For any other dog he meets,
  not even for himself;
Then hide your mats, and put your meat
  upon the topmost shelf.

If you see a little dog,
   barking at the cars,
A raggy dog, a shaggy dog,
   with eyes like twinkling stars,
Just let me know, for though he's bad,
   as bad as bad can be;
I wouldn't change that dog
   for all the treasures of the sea!

                — Emily Lewis

Two Sounds *o* Can Stand For

■Listen for the vowel sound in each of these words as you say it to yourself.

rock   goes   do   corn

Each of those words has the vowel **o** in it.

But no two of those words have the same vowel sound, do they?

The vowel **o** doesn't stand for just one sound.

By itself or with another vowel, it can stand for any one of many sounds.

■Listen for the vowel sound in each of these words as you say it to yourself.

hole   goat   told

The vowel sound you hear in each of those words is the same as the name of the letter **o**, isn't it?

We call that sound the long **o** sound.

Do you hear the long **o** sound in each of these words?

home   road   gold

■ The mouse knows that the boxes with long **o** words on them have delicious cheese in them.

Can you help the mouse find those boxes?

Now listen for the vowel sound in each of these words.

hot   pond   stop

The vowel sound you hear in each of those words is just like the vowel sound in **got**, isn't it?

We call that sound the short **o** sound.

Do you hear the short **o** sound in each of these words?

doggy   rocket

■ The mouse likes corn, too.

Can you help the mouse find the ears of corn with the short **o** words on them?

book

top

open

nose

problem

not

those

lock

153

Parents
Are
People

Mommies are people.

People with children.

When mommies were little

They used to be girls,

Like some of you,

But then they grew.

And now mommies are women,
Women with children,
Busy with children
And things that they do.
There are a lot of things
A lot of mommies can do.

Some mommies are ranchers
Or poetry makers
Or doctors or teachers
Or cleaners or bakers.
Some mommies drive taxis
Or sing on TV.
Yes, mommies can be
Almost anything they want to be.

They can't be grandfathers . . .
Or daddies . . .

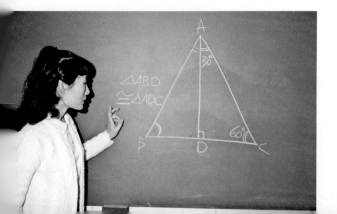

Daddies are people.
People with children.
When daddies were little
They used to be boys,
Like some of you,
But then they grew.

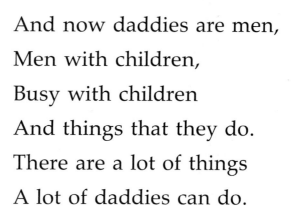

And now daddies are men,
Men with children,
Busy with children
And things that they do.
There are a lot of things
A lot of daddies can do.

Some daddies are writers
Or grocery sellers
Or painters or welders
Or funny joke tellers.
Some daddies play cello
Or sail on the sea.
Yes, daddies can be
Almost anything they want to be.

They can't be grandmas . . .
Or mommies . . .

Parents are people.
People with children.
When parents were little
They used to be children,
Like all of you,
But then they grew.

And now parents are grown-ups,
Grown-ups with children,
Busy with children
And things that they do.
There are a lot of things
A lot of mommies
And a lot of daddies
And a lot of parents
Can do.

— *Carol Hall*

158

Christina Katerina
and the Box

by Patricia Lee Gauch

Christina Katerina liked things.

She liked old dresses.

She liked worn-out ties.

But most of all, she liked boxes.

Bakery boxes, shoe boxes, red boxes, blue boxes.

Best of all she liked great big boxes.

So she was happy one hot day —
when her sometimes-friend Fats Watson
was away — to see a truck come
up to the house with a great, tall box.

In the box was a new freezer.

"Oh, how grand and new,"
Christina's mother said, looking
at the freezer.

"It is! Oh, it really is!"
said Christina, looking at the box.
"I can put it under the apple tree."

To mother, boxes were to throw away,
not for front yards under the apple tree.
But she said it would be all right —
for one day or two.

The Castle

That same day, Christina's father cut
a window and door in the box.

Christina painted on turrets
and a drawbridge.

And the box became a castle.

Inside, she put sticks on the window
for bars.

And she brought in all her dishes,
and some cake, in case there was
a battle and she couldn't get out.

For two days she and her bears played
in her castle, and they were very happy.
Until Fats Watson came home.
He hid in her castle and ate
all the cake when she was out to lunch.

164

When she came back, she wouldn't let him out until he shouted, "I'm sorry" ten times.

When she finally let him out, Fats gave the castle a push and over it went on its side.

The Clubhouse

Mother came out and saw
the fallen cardboard box.
"I see that's the end of the castle,
Christina," she said with a smile
and started to take it away.

"But that's no castle," said Christina,
pulling it back again.
"That's my clubhouse!"

And it was — for three days.
There under the apple tree.

Christina made the window into a door
and the door into a window.

She put in three chairs to sit on.
There were two chairs for the members.
And there was one chair for the president.

Then she painted "Keep out," and
"Members only," on the outside.
And she let Fats be a member.

Then they met in the clubhouse
and said they would be friends forever.
And they were —
until one day Fats got mad
when Christina wouldn't
let him be president.

He climbed on the clubhouse roof
and said he was going to sit there
until Christina did make him president.

Only the roof fell in first
and Christina called off the club.

When Mother saw the sat-in box,
she said, "I see that's the end
of the clubhouse, Christina,"
and she began to take it away.

"But that's no clubhouse,"
said Christina, pulling it back again.
"That's my racing car, Hermione,
and I'm late for a race."

The Racing Car

Christina put the top on the bottom
and turned the window into a cockpit.
On the sides she put two big horns
that she blew at Fats every time
she rounded the apple tree.

170

For two days she raced around the yard
and won every time —
until Fats said he'd take a look
at the motor.

When he cut off the nose
to get at the motor, the car fell apart.

"Well," Christina's mother said,
"that is the end of the racing car,"
and she pulled the cardboard away.

"But that's no racing car,"
said Christina, pulling it back again.
"That's the floor of my home.
And I'm going to have a dance."

And she did.
There under the apple tree.

The Dance Floor

She patted the box out flat
and painted a dance floor on it.
Then she and her bears and Fats
danced and danced.

173

They had a wonderful time —
until Fats decided to wash the floor.
He washed it so much that there was
no floor left.

When Mother came out and saw it,
she asked, "Is this the end
of your grand floor?"

"What floor?" asked Christina,
who was running by.
"Oh, you mean that old box?
Let's do throw it away.
Fats's mother got a washer
and drier today.
And Fats is coming with two ships now.
I said my mother wouldn't mind a bit
if we played with them here —
under the apple tree."

You Do It Too

I can jump, jump, jump
Like a kangaroo,
With a bump, bump, bump.
Can you do it too?

I can creep along
Like a jungle cat.
My steps are long.
Are yours like that?

I can spread my wings
Like a bird in the sky,
And fly 'round in rings —
Would you like to try?

— Margaret Langford

Clues

STORIES

POEMS

INFORMATIONAL ARTICLES

SKILL LESSONS

What Mary Jo Shared

by Janice May Udry

Mary Jo never shared anything
at school.

She was afraid to stand
before the other children and tell
about anything.

She didn't think they would listen.

Almost every day Miss Willet would say,
"Mary Jo, do you have something
to share with us this morning?"

Mary Jo always shook her head
and looked down at her hands.

"Why don't you ever share anything?"
her friend Laurie asked.

"I will some day," said Mary Jo.
"I just don't want to today."
Mary Jo really did want to share,
but she was afraid to try.

Almost every night her father asked,
"Did you share something
at school today?"

"Not today," Mary Jo would say.

One morning it was raining hard.
"I'll share my new umbrella,"
thought Mary Jo as soon as she saw
the rain on the window.

She could hardly wait.
She got ready for school and
ate her breakfast as fast as she could.

Then it was time to put on
her new yellow raincoat and to take
her new yellow umbrella to school.
This was the first umbrella
she had ever owned.

When she got to the school door,
she shook her umbrella and took it inside.

At the door of her room,
she saw many other umbrellas!

"Almost everyone in my room has
an umbrella, too," thought Mary Jo.

"Maybe that isn't a good thing
to share after all."

At Sharing Time, Miss Willet said,
"Mary Jo, do you have something
to share with us this morning?"

Mary Jo shook her head
and looked down.

The next day Mary Jo and her brother
found a grasshopper.

They put it in a can.

The can had holes in the top of it.

"I'll share the grasshopper!"
thought Mary Jo.

And she took the can to school.

When she got to the door of her room,
some children were looking at something
Jimmy had brought.

Mary Jo carefully put her things away.
Then she went to see
what the other children were looking at.

"Jimmy's got five grasshoppers!"
said Laurie.
"He found all of them himself."

Mary Jo thought a bit
about the grasshopper
her brother had helped her get.

"I don't think I will share
my grasshopper after all,"
thought Mary Jo.

At Sharing Time, Miss Willet said,
"Mary Jo, do you have something
to share with us this morning?"

Mary Jo shook her head
and looked down.

Things for Sharing Time

All the other children
in Miss Willet's room shared things.
They shared letters
from their grandmothers
or they shared their pets —
frogs, rabbits, and kittens.
They shared things they found
at the park and things they found
in the woods.

Mary Jo didn't have a grandmother
to get letters from.

She didn't have any pets.

She never found anything at the park
or in the woods that someone
hadn't shared before.

But Mary Jo felt that she just had
to find something to share
that no one in her room had shared.

It got so she could hardly think
of anything but that.

One night Mary Jo had a dream.

In the dream she wanted to share
her new pet elephant.

But when Mary Jo brought
her elephant to Miss Willet's room,
he was too big to squeeze
through the door.
So — in her dream —
she sadly took
her new pet away.

Mary Jo Thinks of Something

"What can I share?" she wondered
over and over.

Her father came home.
"Did you share something at school
today, Mary Jo?" he asked her.

Mary Jo said, "Not today."

Just then Mary Jo thought
of something!
"Could you go to school with me
in the morning?" she asked her father.

"Yes," said her father.

"I don't have to be at school
until ten in the morning."

Mary Jo's father was a teacher
in the high school.

"Good!" said Mary Jo.

"Then you can come
and hear me share something."

"All right," said her father.

"What are you going to share?"

"It's a secret," said Mary Jo.

As soon as Mary Jo and her father
got to school the next morning,
Mary Jo took her father over to Miss Willet.

Miss Willet said she was very happy
to have him visit the room.

"I've got something to share today,"
said Mary Jo.

"Good," said Miss Willet.
"There's the bell."

Mary Jo's father sat by the window
as Miss Willet called all the children's
names to see who was not there.

Then it was Sharing Time.

As soon as Miss Willet asked
if anyone had anything to share,
Mary Jo put up her hand.

"Mary Jo," said Miss Willet.
"You may share with us first
this morning."

Mary Jo stood up and walked
to the front of the room.

"This morning I have brought
my father to share!" she said
with a smile.

This made all the children smile,
and they looked at Mary Jo's father.

He stood, smiled a little
in his friendly way, and waited
to be shared.

"This is my father, Mr. William Wood.

He has a wife and three children.

I am the littlest one," said Mary Jo.

Jimmy put up his hand.

"My father grew up in the West,"
said Jimmy.

"Where did your father grow up?"

"My father came from the West, too,"
said Mary Jo.

"He teaches at the high school."

"He likes to read a lot," Mary Jo went on.
"And he likes to go fishing."

"So does my father!" said Laurie.

"My father puts up houses," said Dan.

"My father visits many places
in his work," said Pam.

They all wanted to share their fathers!
"Children," said Miss Willet,
"it is Mary Jo who is telling us
about her father today.
Please don't make so much noise."

"Before my father grew up,
he was a little boy," said Mary Jo.
Then her face turned hot
because that sounded silly.

All the children laughed.
But Mary Jo went on.
"Sometimes he wasn't too good."

One of the boys asked, "What did he do?"

"One day he locked his little brother
out of the house," said Mary Jo.

"And one day he ate
all the cake his mother had made
for a big school supper."

"Now my father will talk to you,"
she said.

Mr. Wood smiled and talked a bit
about how much he liked visiting
Miss Willet's room.

The children clapped,
and Mary Jo and her father sat down.

Mary Jo felt good.
At last she had shared something
that no one in her room had thought
of sharing.

At Home in the Desert

A desert is a very dry place
with almost no water.

The days are very hot,
and the nights are very cold.

There is little rain.

When it does rain, it rains hard.

But it doesn't rain very long.

It is hard for plants and animals
to live in a desert.

But some animals do know how
to make the desert their home.

All animals must have water to live.
Many desert animals go
to water holes for water.
Animals that do not get water
from water holes or from rain
get it from the things they eat.

Many animals have to stay inside
when the sun is hottest.

Some of them make holes
in the dirt.

Rabbits and foxes live in holes.

Some toads make holes
where they sleep until rain comes.

The rain sometimes washes
the animals' homes away.

The hot sun is a bigger problem
for most desert birds.

Some birds sleep in the daytime
and go hunting at night.

Woodpeckers make holes in plants.
One kind of owl finds a hole
that has been made by another animal
and stays there when the sun is hot.

Some birds must leave the desert
when there is no water.
They go to places where they stay
until it rains in the desert again.

When it rains in the desert,
there are flowers everywhere.

Leaves pop out on trees and bushes.

Soon after the rain ends, the leaves
drop off.

And the desert turns brown again.

Two Sounds *u* Can Stand For

■Listen for the vowel sound in each
of these words as you say it to yourself.

but　　hurt　　push　　suit

Every one of those words has
the vowel **u** in it.

But no two of those words have
the same vowel sound, do they?

The vowel **u** doesn't stand for just
one sound.

By itself or with another vowel, it
can stand for any one of many sounds.

■Listen for the first vowel sound
in **unicorn.**

It sounds just like the name
of the letter **u**, doesn't it?

We call that sound the long **u** sound.

■ Can you find the long **u** words
in these sentences?

The sentences tell
about the dogs in the picture.

Three puppy dogs are in uniforms.
They are pulling a stuck mule.
They are cute, aren't they?

■ Now listen for the vowel sound
in each of these words.

cut   run   truck

The vowel sound in each is just like
the first sound in **us**, isn't it?

We call that sound the short **u** sound.

Do you hear the short **u** sound
in each of these words?

must   jump   club

■ There will be a puppet show.

Only puppets with short **u** words
on them will be in it.

Find those puppets.

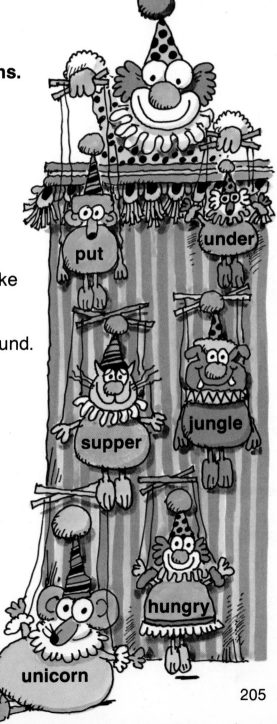

ANIMALS' HOUSES

Of animals' houses
  Two sorts are found —
Those which are square ones
  And those which are round.

Square is a hen-house,
  A kennel, a sty:
Cows have square houses
  And so have I.

A snail's shell is curly,
  A bird's nest round;
Rabbits have twisty burrows
  Underground.

But the fish in the bowl
  And the fish at sea —
Their houses are round
  As a house can be.

                    — *James Reeves*

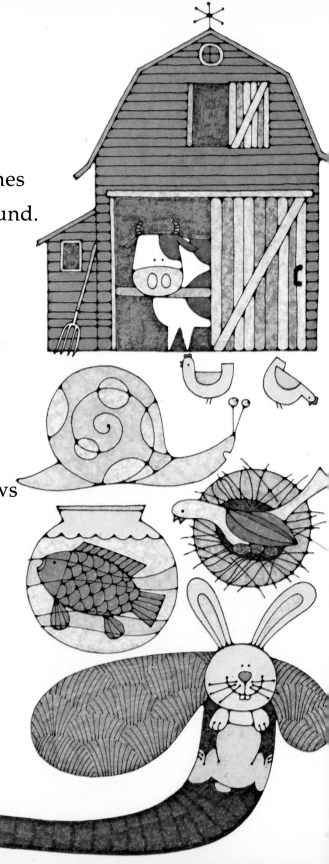

Nate the Great

by Marjorie Weinman Sharmat

My name is Nate the Great.

I am a detective.

Let me tell you about my last case:

I had just eaten breakfast.

It was a good breakfast.

Pancakes and milk and pancakes.

I like pancakes.

I heard the telephone.

It was Annie.

Annie lives down the street.

"I lost a picture," Annie said.

"Can you help me find it?"

"Of course," I said.

"I have found lost balls, books, shoes, rabbits.

Even a lost goldfish.

Now I, Nate the Great, will find a lost picture."

"Oh, good," Annie said.
"When can you come over?"

"I will be over in five minutes,"
I said.
"Stay right where you are.
Don't touch anything.
DON'T MOVE!"

I put on my detective hat and took
my notebook.

I left a note for my mother.
I always leave a note for my mother
when I am on a case.

Annie's House

I went to Annie's house.

Annie has brown hair and brown eyes.

And she smiles a lot.

She was eating breakfast.

Pancakes.

"I like pancakes," I said.

It was a good breakfast.

"Tell me about your picture," I said.

"I painted a picture of my dog, Fang," Annie said.

"I put it on my desk to dry.

Then it was gone.

It happened yesterday."

"You should have called me yesterday," I said, "when the trail was hot.

I hate cool trails.

Now, where would a picture go?"

"I don't know," Annie said.

"That's why I called you.

Are you sure you're a detective?"

"Sure, I'm sure.

I will find the picture of Fang,"
I said.

"Tell me.

Does this house have

any secret passages?"

"No," Annie said.

"No secret passages?" I said.
"This will be a very dull case.
Now show me your room."

We went to Annie's room.
It was big.
It had yellow walls, a yellow bed,
a yellow chair, and a yellow desk.

I, Nate the Great, was sure
of one thing.
Annie liked yellow.

I looked all over the room.

I looked on the desk.

And under the desk.

And in the desk.

No picture.

I looked on the bed.

And under the bed.

And in the bed.

I looked in the wastebasket.
I found a picture of a dog.

"Is this it?" I asked.

"No," Annie said.
"My picture of Fang is yellow."

"I should have known," I said.

The Real Fang

"Now tell me.
Who has seen your picture?"

"My friend Rosamond has seen it,
and my brother Harry.
And Fang."

"Tell me about Fang," I said.
"Is he a big dog?"

"Very big," Annie said.

"Does he have big teeth?" I asked.

"Very big," Annie said.

"Does he bite people?" I asked.

"No," Annie said.
"Will this help the case?"

"No," I said.
"But it may help me.
Show me Fang."

Annie took me out to the yard.

Fang was there.

He was big, all right.

And he had big teeth.

He showed them to me.

I showed him my teeth.

He sniffed me.

I sniffed him back.

And we were friends.

220

I watched him with a bone.

"Hmm," I said.

"Watch Fang bury that bone.

He buries very well.

He could bury other things.

Like a picture."

"Why would he bury a picture?"
Annie asked.

"Maybe it wasn't a good picture
of him," I said.

"I never thought of that," said Annie.

I, Nate the Great, think of everything.

"Tell me," I said.

"Does Fang ever leave this yard?"

"Only with me," said Annie.

"I see," I said.

"Then the only place he could bury
the picture is in the yard.
Come."

Annie and I dug for a long time.

We found rocks, bones, and ants.
But no picture.

At last I stood up.

I, Nate the Great, had something
to say.

"I am hungry."

"Would you like some more pancakes?"
Annie asked.

I could tell that Annie was
a smart girl.

We sat in the kitchen.

Cold pancakes are almost as good
as hot pancakes.

Rosamond's House

"Now, on with the case," I said.
"Next we will talk to your friend
Rosamond."

Annie and I walked to Rosamond's house.
Rosamond had black hair and green eyes.
And cat hair all over her.

"I am Nate the Great," I said.
"I am a detective."

"A detective?" said Rosamond.
"A real, live detective?"

"Touch me," I said.

"How do I know you are a detective?"
asked Rosamond.
"Find something.
Find my lost cat."

"I am on a case," I said.
"I am on a big case."

"My lost cat is big," Rosamond said.

"His name is Super Hex.

Here are my other cats — " Big Hex,

Little Hex, and Plain Hex."

The cats had black hair and green eyes.

We went into Rosamond's house.

I looked around.

There were cat pictures everywhere.

We sat down.

Little Hex jumped onto Annie's lap.

Plain Hex jumped onto Rosamond's lap.

Big Hex jumped onto my lap.

I did not like Big Hex.

Big Hex did not like me.

"Time to go," I said.

"We just got here," Annie said.

She liked Little Hex.

"Time to go," I said again.

I stood up.

I tripped over something.

It was long and black.

It was a cat's tail.

"MEOW!"

"Super Hex!" Rosamond cried.

"You found him!

You are a detective."

"Of course," I said.

"He was under my chair.

Except for his tail."

Annie and I left.

It was a hard thing to do.

I could smell pancakes

in Rosamond's kitchen.

"Rosamond did not take the picture

of your dog," I said.

"Rosamond only likes cats.

And pancakes.

Now where is your brother Harry?"

Harry's Room

I met Annie's brother.

He was small.

He was covered with red paint.

"Me paint," he said.

"Me paint you."

"Good," I said.

"No one has ever painted a picture of me, Nate the Great."

Harry took his paintbrush.
It was covered with red paint.
All at once I was covered
with red paint.

"He painted you," Annie said.
"He painted you."
Then she laughed.

I, Nate the Great, did not laugh.
I was on a case.
I had a job to do.

I looked around the room.

Harry had really painted!

There were pictures of a clown,
a house, and a tree.

There was a picture of a monster
with three heads.

He had painted some of the wall,
one shoe, and part of the door.

"He does very good work," I said.

"But where is my picture?"
Annie asked.

Where <u>was</u> the picture of Fang?
I could not find it.
Fang did not have it.
Rosamond did not have it.
Harry did not have it.
Or did he?

All at once I knew I had found the lost picture.

I said, "I, Nate the Great, have found your picture."

"You have?" Annie said. "Where?"

"Look!" I said.
"Harry has a picture of a clown, a house, a tree, and a monster with three heads."

"So what?" Annie said.

"Look again," I said.

"The picture of the clown is red.

The picture of the house is red.

The picture of the tree is red.

But the picture of the monster is orange."

"So what?" Annie said again.
"Orange is great for a monster."

"But Harry paints with *red*," I said.
"Everything is red but the monster.
I, Nate the Great, will tell you why.
Harry painted a red monster
over the yellow picture of your dog.
The yellow paint was still wet.
It mixed with the red paint.
Yellow and red make orange.
That is why the monster is orange."

Annie opened her mouth.
She did not say a word.
Then she closed her mouth.

I said, "See!

The monster has three heads.

Two of the heads were your dog's ears.

The other head was the tail.

Yes, he <u>does</u> do good work."

Annie was very mad at her brother.

I was mad, too.

I, Nate the Great, had never been

red before.

"This case is done," I said.

"I must go."

A Happy Ending

"I don't know how to thank you,"
Annie said.

"I do," I said.
"Are there any pancakes left?"

I hate to eat on the job.
But the job was over.

We sat in Annie's kitchen.
Annie and I.
And Harry.

Annie said, "I will paint
a new picture.
Will you come back to see it?"

"If Harry doesn't see it first,"
I said.

Annie smiled.
Harry smiled.
They even smiled at each other.

I smiled, too.

I, Nate the Great, like happy endings.

It was time to leave.

I said good-by to Annie and Harry and Fang.

I started to walk home.

Rain started to fall.

I was glad I had my rubbers.

TROLL TRICK

With many a scowl
And many a frown,
A troll pushed
Stones and boulders down.

The crashing sound
Made town folks wonder:
Is it a troll
Or is it thunder?

But hill folks knew.
When boulders roll,
It's always the trick
Of a terrible troll.

— B. J. Lee

Copyright 1970 by Leland B. Jacobs

The
Shoelaces

by Tony Johnston

One day the new spring greens were
on the trees, and Mole had on new shoes.

"Troll," he called.

"Yoo-hoo, Troll.

I have new shoes.

Aren't they the best shoes

you've ever seen?"

"They are neat," said Troll.

"But why don't you tie the laces?"

"I don't know how," said Mole.

"Here is how," said Troll.

He tied the laces in a neat bow.

"Thank you very much," said Mole.

"Don't mention it," said Troll.

"Now we can stroll through the fields."

Mole and Troll strolled
through the sunny mushroom fields.

Mole looked down at his new shoes
in the sun.

The laces were untied.

"Troll," he said.

"Yes, Mole?"

"Will you do me a little favor?"

"Anything," said Troll.

"Will you tie my laces again?
They have come untied from our strolling."
Mole sat down on a mushroom, and Troll
tied the laces in a neat bow.

"There," Troll said.

"Now we can finish our stroll."

"Oh, thank you," said Mole.

"Don't mention it," said Troll.

They had gone just a little farther
when — bump.

Mole tripped on his shoelaces
and fell down flat.

"Are you all right?" asked Troll.

"Fine," said Mole.
"But will you do me a little favor?"

"Sure," said Troll.

"Will you tie my laces?
They have come untied again," said Mole.

"I would love to tie them again,"
said Troll.

Mole sat down on another mushroom
and Troll tied the laces
in a nice, neat bow.

"Thank you, Troll," said Mole.

"I wish you wouldn't mention it,"
said Troll.
He was getting cross.

Then they went through a foxtail field.
Mole was making some scissors
when — boink!
He tripped and fell into some foxtails.

"Ouch!" Mole cried.

"Are you all right?" asked Troll.

"Just fine," grumbled Mole.

"But these laces are not all right.

They are dangerous.

Will you please tie them tight?"

Troll was very cross.

He said, "I am not a shoe clerk.

I am a troll.

Why should I tie laces all day long

when I do not even wear shoes!

You tie the laces!"

Mole Ties His Own Laces

So Mole tied the laces.

He tied them and tied them
and tied them.

He really knotted them.

He knotted them
in a triple clove-hitch knot.

"There," he said.

"Now they are on good and tight."

"Yes," said Troll.

"Now they are on forever."

Mole looked worried.

"Forever?" he said.

"Forever," said Troll.

"A triple clove-hitch knot is the same
as forever."

"Will I have to wear my shoes
in the bathtub?" asked Mole.

"Yes," said Troll.

"In bed?" asked Mole.

"Yes," said Troll.

"At the beach?" asked Mole.

"Forever," said Troll.

Mole started to cry.
He liked his new shoes.
But he did not want them on FOREVER.

Just then a robin hopped by.

She had been eyeing the laces
for some time.

"Pretty nice shoelaces you got there,"
she said.

"They are all knotted up!" cried Mole.
"Who wants them?"

"I do," said the robin, "for my nest."

"Then take them!" cried Mole.

The robin untied the laces easily
and flew off singing.
She left the shoes.
And Mole and Troll
strolled home happily.

After the Rain is Over

After the sky
is bright again,
after the rain is over,
it's easy to tell
where the wind has been—
smelling the wild sweet clover!
Smelling so hard
and smelling so well
the air is flooded
with clover smell.

—Aileen Fisher